Series / Number 04-008

A Theory of Political Coalitions in Simple and Policymaking Situations

PAUL T. HILL
National Institute of Education

SAGE PUBLICATIONS / Beverly Hills / London

For information address:

SAGE PUBLICATIONS, INC.
275 South Beverly Drive
Beverly Hills, California 90212

SAGE PUBLICATIONS, INC.
St George's House / 44 Hatton Garden
London EC1N 8ER

International Standard Book Number 0-8039-0306-5

Library of Congress Catalog Card No. L.C. 73-87851

FIRST PRINTING

When citing a professional paper, please use the proper form. Remember to cite the
correct Sage Professional Paper series title and include the paper number. One of the
two following formats can be adapted (depending on the style manual used):

(1) NAGEL, S. S. (1973) "Comparing Elected and Appointed Judicial Systems."
Sage Professional Paper in American Politics, 1, 04-001. Beverly Hills and London:
Sage Pubns.

OR

(2) Nagel, Stuart S. 1973. *Comparing Elected and Appointed Judicial Systems.* Sage
Professional Paper in American Politics, vol. 1. no. 04-001. Beverly Hills and London:
Sage Publications.

CONTENTS

A Theory of Political Coalitions in Simple and Policymaking Situations

PAUL T. HILL
National Institute of Education

Despite the recent growth in the volume and sophistication of coalition theory, the literature still lacks a unifying framework. Three distinct theoretical models, each with its own vocabulary and mode of explanation, have been used to develop coalition theory. They are: the mathematical-normative model, which derives "rational" solutions to conflict situations; the economic—cost-benefit model, which explains coalition formation in terms of cost-benefit calculations, and the social-psychological model, which explains coaltion formation in terms of actors' calculations of their own personal advantage.

Though each model is responsible for some unique contributions, the overlap in their fundamental content is considerable. The commonalities suggest that it should be possible to synthesize the insights of the three models into a single comprehensive theory. Such is the work of this monograph. It uses a single explanatory model, the social-psychological, to produce a theory which integrates the basic insights of the existing literature, and provides a structure to guide further inquiry.

The new theory concentrates on explaining three aspects of coalition formation—the total resources of the winning coalition, the allocation of rewards among members of the winning coalition, and the establishment of coalition "policies" which affect the allocation of goods, rights, or

AUTHOR'S NOTE: *The author wishes to acknowledge many helpful suggestions from Professors Philip Burgess, John Kessell, and Richard Hoffstetter in the preparation of early drafts of this monograph.*

obligations among persons outside the coalition situation. The theory explains these outcomes in terms of the direct effects and interactions of such independent variables as the completeness of information available to actors, the complexity of the situation, the continuity of the decision-making group, and uncertainty about the requisite characteristics of a winning coalition.

The theory distinguishes the dynamics of "simple" coalition situations —those whose only outcomes are payoffs to members of the winning coalition—and "policy-making" situations.

I. INTRODUCTION AND DEFINITIONS

Interest in serious theoretical and empirical study of political coalition formation has grown steadily in the past few years. The body of research literature is now receiving an unprecedented number of additions.

Despite the adherence of most of the contributors to scientific norms the coalition literature has yet to achieve an integrated vocabulary, a generally accepted methodology, or a consensus on the most useful conceptual framework. Coalition theory has been advanced through various techniques, including adaptations of game theory, economic analysis, and experimental psychology. The result of this profusion of methodologies and conceptual statements is that the several findings and theoretical statements are not cumulative. Though each contribution is valuable, the whole does not add up to a theory or even a theoretical tradition. The proliferation of approaches to coalition formation has, moreover, prevented the development of a parsimonious and internally consistent body of concepts. This lack of theoretical unity is not necessary, for even though the theories are conceptualized differently, (i.e., the theorists use different conceptual models and have not attempted integrative and synthetic statements) there is substantial overlap in the topics covered. And though different models lead to different operational difinitions, many of the models incorporate virtually identical variables.

This paper will identify and exploit those commonalities in an effort to produce a single theoretical model which will integrate the insights of existing coalition theories and expand the range of their explanatory power.

The value of such an effort is clear only in the context of a review of the existing theories and their related research findings. The following section presents that review.

TERMINOLOGY

In order to facilitate the review, it will be useful to develop a basic vocabulary, which can be used in lieu of the disparate terminologies associated with particular theories and theorists. The following glossary should be adequate:

Coalition situation: A coalition situation is defined by the existence of a political decision-making group.

A political decision-making group[1] has the following characteristics:

(1) It controls access to certain goods or privileges which all actors desire.

(2) At least some of the goods it controls are scarce, i.e. they cannot be enjoyed simultaneously to the full satisfaction of all actors.

(3) No single actor can control the allocation of those goods.

(4) Some accepted procedure for determining the allocation of those goods exists.

(5) Those procedures permit the scarce goods to be allocated unequally among actors by agreement of less than the entire membership

A coalition is two or more participants in a group of three or more actors who coordinate the use of their resources in controlling or attempting to control a decision.

A winning coalition is a coalition which is large enough to determine the allocation of rewards among all members of the decision-making group.

When it is not certain whether a decision can truly alter the allocation of rewards among members of the decision-making group (for example, in cases where the group must compete with other groups in order to obtain the rewards) a coalition large enough to determine the allocation of any potential rewards is a controlling coalition.

A minimal winning (or controlling) coalition is a coalition which would no longer be winning (or controlling) if it lost any unit of resources.

Payoff is the benefit which a member of the winning coalition derives directly from membership in the winning coalition. Payoff is distinct from reward. Members of the winning coalition may wish to extend some benefits to participants who are not members of the winning coalition in order, for example, to keep the decision-making group together. Hence, reward is the absolute value of benefits enjoyed by any participant; it is distinct from payoff, which is the benefit accruing only to members of the winning coalition.[2]

An actor in a coalition situation is a person who holds resources which are directly useful in making a decision.

A participant is an actor who is in the process of seeking membership in a winning coalition.

A member of a winning coalition is a participant who has joined with one or more others to form a winning coalition.

Decision-making groups can be classified according to the number of decisions they make. A terminal group makes a single decision and disbands. A continuing group makes more than one decision before disbanding.

There are two kinds of decisions. A simple decision changes the allocation of goods or privileges only among members of the decision-making group. A policy decision commits the group to some action or statement intended to affect the behavior of persons who are not members of the decision-making group, or to affect the allocation of goods, privileges, or obligations among persons who are not members of the decision-making group. Though it is possible for a decision-making group to make a simple decision without making policy, the nature of coalition decision-making requires that policy decisions always imply simple decisions.

The nature of resources depends on the rules of the decision-making group. In conventions, committees, and legislatures, resources are formally defined as votes. (This definition deliberately excludes behind-the-scenes operators, who do not have resources but who have access to persons who do, from the status of actors.)

II. THE LITERATURE

In order to set the context for the rest of the paper this review shall proceed in two distinct steps. The first will be to identify and examine exemplars of the three chief theoretical models found in the coalition literature and to assess their respective advantages and limitations in explaining coalition behavior. The second step will be to integrate all of the theoretical models around the chief dependent variables which most of the theories attempt to explain. The discussion will procede as follows:

I. The Chief Theoretical Models
   A. Mathematical–normative
   B. Economic–cost-benefit
   C. Social–Psychological

I. THE CHIEF THEORETICAL MODELS

A. Mathematical–Normative

The mathematical–normative tradition in coalition theory is founded on Von Neumann and Morgenstren's (1964) theory of games. Game theory uses mathematical analysis to discover "rational" outcomes for conflict situations.

(In a conflict situation, enough rewards are available to satisfy some, but not all actors. A rational outcome is one which produces the greatest possible rewards for those actors who can control the situation.)

Because actors in conflict situations can order their preferences among possible outcomes, it is possible to determine which of any pair of outcomes is preferred by a majority of participants. In a pair of possible outcomes, the more preferred dominates the other. Out of all possible pairs of outcomes, there will be a core set of outcomes, each of which dominates at least one other outcome and is not itself dominated by any other outcome.

The set of undominated outcomes can be computed objectively, assuming only (a) that all participants share a single definition of a desirable outcome as one which maximizes personal payoff, and (b) that all participants can exactly compute the payoffs accruing to themselves from any possible outcome.

Game theory is thus mathematical because it deals with payoffs and preferences as abstract quantities and normative because it specifies which outcomes should occur if participants behave rationally.

Political coalition situations are a subclass of the conflict situations encompassed by game theory for they are typically "constant-sum" games, i.e., the total payoff from the solution of any conflict is fixed, and does not vary according to the number or identities of participants on the winning side. For constant sum situations game theory provides an important insight: participants wishing to maximize their personal payoffs can do so by minimizing others' claims on the fixed payoff, i.e., by forming the smallest possible winning coalition. This insight is the basis for mathematical–normative theories of political coalition formation.

A number of researchers have used the vocabulary and insights of game theory to generate propositions about political coalition formation. Perhaps the most influential of these has been William Riker.

Though Riker (1962a: 23) recognized that natural political settings seldom permit the unambiguous calculations of personal interest assumed by game theory, he tried to apply game theory's insights to political coalition behavior with as little change as possible. The result was what Riker has called the size principle:

> In social situations similar to n-person zero-sum games with side-payments, participants create coalitions just as large as they believe will insure winning, and no larger.

Riker (1962a) presents several kinds of evidence for the size principle. Historic events, ranging from convention decisions to international alliance agreements, are shown to be consistent with the size principle.

In another work Riker (1965) supplies more rigorous mathematical proofs.

As an effort to transfer a powerful insight from a mathematical theory to a predictive-explanatory statement about real social phenomena, the size principle is valuable. But it is restricted, in its current form, to a vivid statement of one process of many operating simultaneously in complex natural coalition situations.

The principle is limited for a number of reasons. First, it is not stated in a way that leads itself to easy measurement. To apply or extrapolate from the size principle, the observer must judge for himself whether a situation is similar enough to an n-person zero-sum game with side-payments to permit the application of the size principle. If the observer avoids subjective judgment by applying the size principle only in conditions where it applies unequivocally, he faces the second limitation. He is restricted to n-person zero-sum games in which all players are rational and have perfect and complete information. Riker himself has commented that such situations are too rare in the natural world to make a theory about them very useful.

A second mathematically-based political coalition theory is presented by Michael Leiserson (1968) in the context of his study of coalitions and factions in the Japanese Liberal Democratic Party. Operationally, Leiserson's adaptation of game theory is not much different from Riker's: he simply hypothesizes—and confirms—that Cabinet selection in the Japanese Diet is close enough to an n-person zero-sum game with side-payments to promote formation of minimal winning coalitions.

He does elaborate on game theory with two new propositions—one predicting that winning coalitions will tend to be minimal in number of members as well as total resources, and the other predicting that coalitions meant to be long-lasting will be formed with slightly greater than minimal resources—but these innovations are based on essentially nonmathematical rationale. They do help to broaden the range of situations to which the theory applies, but they do not solve the problems of operationalization raised in discussing Riker's theory.

Brams and Riker (1970) and Brams and Heilman (1971) use mathematical techniques to investigate the process by which coalition formation outcomes predicted by Riker's and other theories are achieved. Their analysis is based on the addition which each individual makes to a protocoalition's probability of becoming a winning coalition. They employ probability lattices to provide visual representation of the incremental addition that each new member makes to a protocoalition's chances of winning.

The lattice presentation indicates that new members' incremental additions vary from one stage of the process to another. The addition a given weight of resources affects a coalition's chances of winning differently at different stages of the coalition's growth. Assuming that members of a winning coalition are rewarded in proportion to their contribution to the coalition's chance of winning, the authors can predict the time at which a participant is most likely to commit himself.

Though their analysis adds little to our understanding of the likely composition of a winning coalition, it does produce some interesting hypotheses about the timing of participants' choices of coalitions and their expectations of rewards should the coalition win. We shall treat those contributions in section II.

B. Economic

The economic or "cost-benefit" coalition theory model is also closely related to game theory; it extends game theory by considering additional aspects of coalition forming situations.

A number of economists and political scientists have added considerations of decision costs to game theory's concentration on payoff maximization. In the decision cost model, payoff is only one factor which a participant in a coalition situation considers. In devising a coalition-forming strategy the rational participant must look at his costs, as well as the resultant benefits. Truly rational behavior lies in maximizing net payoff, the benefits remaining from a decision after the costs of making the decision and living with its consequences are discounted, which is typically less than gross payoff.

Adrian and Press (1968) identify eight categories of decision costs. In general, increases in decision costs increase the likelihood of formation of a larger-than-minimal coalition. A listing and explanation of the cost categories will help to distinguish the economic from the mathematical model.

(1) Information costs: the costs of collecting information about available strategies, of communicating about preference orderings, and of making proposals. High information costs militate against the formation of minimal coalitions.

(2) Responsibility costs: the costs to a person or group of having a policy decision attributed to them. These vary with the size of the winning coalition (responsibility is diluted as the winning coalition grows), with the importance of the policy (grave matters place higher individual and collective responsibility), and with the need to increase the impact of a decision on the constituency (decisions on controversial matters gain legitimacy from large winning coalitions). In general, high responsibility costs encourage formation of larger-than-minimal coalitions.

(3) Intergame costs: the effects of behavior in the present coalition situation on costs in future situations. High intergame costs reduce flexibility in the present, and thus work against the formation of a minimal winning coalition.

(4) Division of payoff costs: the costs involved in distributing payoffs among members of the winning coalition. In situations where total payoff for the winning coalition is a fixed amount, division of payoff costs increase with the addition of each member to a winning coalition. Thus, division of payoff costs encourage formation of minimal winning coalitions.

(5) Dissonance costs: costs of disagreement in decision-making groups which make policy. In cases where all participants have equal resources, dissonance costs are lowest when the number of members of the winning coalition is kept to a minimum. Adrian and Press do not examine the more complex cases such as conventions where delegation heads control blocs of votes where participants have unequal resources.

(6) Inertia costs: the costs of changing existing coalition partnerships. These are essentially the same as intergame costs.

(7) Time costs: The time required to explore all available coalitions. These might also be called effort or opportunity costs: as full exploration of alternative strategies becomes more costly, the likelihood of forming a minimal winning coalition is reduced.

(8) Persuasion costs: the cost of bringing a reluctant member into a coalition. Persuasion costs exist because no participant will enter into a coalition that promises him nothing, and potential coalition members must be offered some share of the winning coalition payoff.

These costs are obviously important to a participant. Very high decision costs (e.g., an intergame cost that made a participant unable to compete successfully in the future for future payoffs) might outweigh the prospect of a high payoff from a single decision. Conversely, a low-cost strategy (e.g., joining the first available winning coalition in order to save time) might bring a higher net payoff than a high cost strategy (e.g., a careful search for alternatives) which makes only marginal improvements in payoff.

It may be reasonably argued that game theory really encompasses decision costs (1) by recognizing their existence but assuming that they are negligible or (2) by assuming that payoff really means net, rather than gross, benefits from a decision. Neither of these arguments really avoids the conclusion that economic cost-benefit analysis makes a distinct and important contribution. The first argument leaves game theory models unable to deal with situations where decision costs are non-negligible. And the second concedes that game theory is inadequate to identify and specify some of the important dynamics of participants' calculations of their own best advantage in coalition situations.

Though the economic model makes a distinct contribution, it shares many of game theory's limitations. It explains a broader array of coalition situations, but an inspection of the decision cost literature reveals that most of it is still concerned with specification of variables and verbal discussion of hypotheses. It has not led to any operational definitions or hypothesis testing, except in descriptive post facto analyses of illustrative natural situations.

The decision cost analysts' operational problems are immense: unlike the game theory model, which requires only one scale to measure benefits, economic analysis must develop measuring scales for each of its cost categories and devise means for making the discrete cost scales comparable among themselves *and* with payoff measurements. This has not been done. However, as we shall discuss later, the insights of decision-cost analysis can be transformed into more easily operationable terms in a theory which is compatible with the insights also of game theory and those of the following model, the social-psychological.

C. Social-Psychological

The third basic model is difficult to define cleanly. The theories based on the social-psychological model vary widely in the scope of explanation they attempt. They have in common an interest in explaining coalition forming behavior as a result of specific modes of cognitive processing (psychological) or as the result of the interaction of group behaviors and individual cognitions (sociological).

Opening coalition theory to a wide array of cognitive and social-interactive variables makes this model far less elegant than the mathematical one. But, despite the lack of elegance, it is possible to transfer the basic insights of the mathematical and economic models to this mode of explanation without sustaining great losses of rigor, and with considerable gains in generality and operationability.

To do so, it is necessary only to examine the implicit assumptions which link any mathematically based theory to predictions about human behavior. Theories like Riker's (1962b) assume a direct relationship between the objective facts of the coalition situation (i.e., the facts that each participant has a determinate quantity of decision-making resources, and that his own payoff is related to the importance of those resources in forming the winning coalition) and the participants' actual adoption of the optimal or minimum winning coalition strategy. The link between the availability of an optimal strategy and a participant's adopting it is so tight that we forget to make it explicit: participants follow the optimal (minimum winning coalition) strategy because they perceive the consequences of different coalition-forming strategies and, preferring a greater payoff to a lesser one, form minimum winning coalitions.

Thus, for example, where Riker's theory makes predictions about human behavior it is basically a statement about the manner in which a participant will understand and respond to a coalition situation. It is, then, little more than a matter of semantics to reformulate the size principle as a statement about the psychological dynamics of a participant in a coalition situation. In making such a reformulation, we reap a major research benefit: it is now possible to see the conditions which Riker specifies for his theory—zero-sum game, full information, and rationality—as extreme values of crucial endogenous variables, rather than as absolute criteria for determining whether a situation is relevant to coalition theory. Zero-sumness, information, and rationality can be treated as variables whose existence depends on a participant's cognitions and behavior, i.e., dependent on their own strength and the strength of other variables which enter into the participant's calculations. Formulated as a psychological calculation of advantage, Riker's size principle need not be limited to the rare instances in which postulated conditions are met.[3]

Gamson (1961a, 1961b) transforms the mathematical insights into social and psychological terms: his hypothesis that participants will form minimal coalitions is based on the expectation that participants will perceive and act upon the implications of the objective mathematical properties of the coalition situation.

Gamson is not the only social-psychological theorist to adapt insights generated under the mathematical-normative model. Chertkoff (1966), for one, makes an original contribution by considering conditions in which participants may employ unusual definitions of winning and maximizing payoff and may therefore behave rationally in a way other than that predicted by the game theorists.

Chertkoff's research considered a very important class of situations, i.e., that in which no possible coalition can be certain of winning the ultimate payoff (for example a Presidential nominating convention.) The formation of a controlling coalition determines which participants *can* be winners, but doesn't absolutely guarantee the payoff to any coalition.

Chertkoff created laboratory situations in which he could observe the effects of uncertainty of winning on coalition formation. He found that the likelihood of winning had a strong effect on participants' choices of coalitions. That effect was independent of coalition size. Between coalitions of equal size participants chose the one with the greatest likelihood of winning; between coalitions whose probability of winning was equal, participants chose the one with least resources.

This finding, as we have said, is relevant to a highly important set of natural coalition situations. It was not included except as Adrian and Press' "Intergame Costs" in any of the mathematical or economic models, but Chertkoff interprets it in a way consistent with both: in such a case "payoff" is really a joint function of the probability of winning and the value of what may be won. Under this new definition, participants who choose the coalition most likely to win have made the rational choice. The prediction of rational behavior is not remarkable but finding it in an important new place is made possible by a theoretical model that relies on human cognition and calculations of advantage to explain behavior.

A number of researchers have employed the social-psychological model in identifying and testing entirely new independent variables to explain coalition forming behavior. Vinacke (1959) for example, found that friendship affects choices of coalition partners, and more among female participants in coalition situations than among males. Festinger and Hoffmann (1954) found that participants prefer joining with others whose decisional resources are similar to their own, even when their combined resources are greater than the optimal (minimal) coalition's. Gamson (1961) and Leiserson (1970) considered situations in which winning coalitions make policy as well as distribute rewards and concluded that policy considerations sometimes help participants choose among coalitions that offer equal payoff.

These findings do not rely on notions of rationality adapted from other models. They involve variables that could only fit in a model that used cognitions and hypothesized intra-psychic processes to explain behavior.

Users of the social-psychological model have generally been more successful than most others in integrating a large number of variables into their theories and have consequently been able to treat a wider range of natural political situations. But those advantages have not been fully exploited. The social-psychological theories have serious shortcomings in three respects:

(1) Most theories have remained on the conceptual level. Despite a great deal of effort in developing the social-psychological model, few of the key concepts have been operationalized well enough to permit standard measurement across studies.

(2) Efforts to quantify absolute and relative effects of independent variables have been weak. This is particularly true in the case of policy-making situations, as we shall see later in this chapter.

(3) Few theories based on the social-psychological models have investigated the interactions among their chief independent variables. Most hypotheses are stated—and the empirical investigations, when conducted at all, are designed—in terms of single-variable effects. This is understandable in the early states of theory-development, but it is a deficiency that must be remedied.

This exposition is sufficient to identify the chief modes of explanation used in coalition theory, to explain some major exemplars of each, and to review their strengths and weaknesses. The next section does the real work of this review, by discussing the ways in which users of each of the basic models have approached the central questions about coalition behavior, and considering the complementarities, overlaps, and gaps among the existing theories.

II. EXPLANATION OF MAJOR DEPENDENT VARIABLES

Despite the fact that theories based on the various models have important differences in predictive range and operational meanings, they generally share certain basic concerns. Exploring the manners in which the various authors attempt to explain those dependent variables will illustrate both the gaps among the theories and the prospects for integrating insights from the various theories.

The chief classes of dependent variables are:

A. Identities of members of the winning coalition.

B. How rewards will be allocated among members of the winning coalition.

C. What tradeoffs will be made between payoff and non-utilitarian strategy preferences.

D. Cohesion and changes in coalition membership over time.

E. What policy the coalition will make once it is formed.

Of the five classes of variables, only the first three are directly related to coalition formation. Because our present concern is with coalition formation rather than with the behavior of coalitions once they are formed, the review will be confined to the three classes of dependent variables which are clearly related to coalition formation.

A. Identity of Members of the Winning Coalition

The identification of members is the main feature of nearly all coalition theories. Despite differences in conceptualization, many of the theories make identical predictions of behavior. Riker and Gamson, as we have seen, make the same prediction—that winning coalitions will have minimal resources—and for reasons that differ only in their manner of presentation.

In terms of the first part of this chapter, Leiserson mixes his models: he adopts the game theory hypothesis of minimal coalitions, but adds a further proposition—that winning coalitions will be minimal in terms of the number of members as well as in total resources. This proposition adds nothing when all participants' resources are equal; but when they are unequal, and more than one minimal-resource coalition is possible, Leiserson predicts that coalitions will be formed of the smallest possible number of members, invoking a "bargaining proposition" based on economic rationale. A minimal coalition of fewer members involves less bargaining cost than a coalition of many members.

Others use very different rationales. Caplow (1956), for example, explains coalition formation as a process of seeking dominance over others: participants wish to leave others of greater resources than themselves out of the winning coalition—the coalition which most nearly achieves this for a winning margin of members will be formed. As Gamson (1961) and Leiserson (1968) show, this explanation leads to unique predictions in some cases.

Gamson (1964) has discussed many theorists who predict greater-than-minimal coalitions. These predictions, however, are not really contrary to the theories predicting minimal coalitions. They simply identify variables—such as anticompetitive norms, confusion, time pressure, and lack of information—which make participants unlikely to establish what Curry (1971) has called "the coalition pattern of interaction." As Curry has demonstrated, hypotheses about coalition-formation behavior are appropriate only when participants are able to perceive an advantage in reducing the payoffs of other participants by coalescing against them.

A number of theorists discuss variables which lead to formation of larger-than-minimal coalitions. Chertkoff deals with situations in which a minimal controlling coalition may be less likely to win the payoff than a larger-than-minimal coalition. If controlling coalitions vary in their likelihood of winning the payoff, Chertkoff's data indicate that the coalition most likely to win, regardless of its size, will be formed.

Gamson (1961a) introduced the concept of nonutilitarian strategy preferences, i.e., considerations other than desire for payoff that affect participants' coalition-forming decisions. These preferences (such as a liking for individual participants, or opinion similarity) affect the choice of partners within the same payoff class: Gamson predicts that nonutilitarian strategy preferences affect the identity of members of the winning coalition only when they cost nothing in terms of payoff. Leiserson (1970) makes a similar prediction about the impact of ideology on coalition formation.[4] Adrian and Press' paper on decision costs identifies a number of variables which tend to increase the size of winning coalitions. Their theoretical statements make explicit some hypotheses which are implied or assumed in other theories.

One such hypothesis is that intergame costs—implications for future decisions of actions taken in the present decision—lead to formation of larger-than-minimal coalitions. This is analogous to hypotheses advanced by Leiserson (1968) and Chertkoff (1966). Participants acting according to Leiserson's "maintenance" hypothesis (i.e., hedging against defections by forming larger-than-minimal coalitions) are simply reacting to the fact that some payoffs are accumulated over an extended length of time. Likewise, Chertkoff's hypothesis that participants "hedge" by forming large coalitions in cases where no coalition is fully certain to win reflects the fact that a single act of coalition formation may not completely determine the distribution of payoffs. The underlying dimension touched upon by Leiserson, Chertkoff, and Adrian and Press (1968) is the completeness of the decision: when the current choice of coalition partners does not wholly determine the ultimate distribution of payoffs, the decision is incomplete. The rational participant may deliberately choose a larger-than-minimal winning coalition.

Adrian and Press also discuss "time costs" and "information cost"—classes of variables that prevent exploration of alternative strategies and make full rational calculation of advantage difficult. In general, lack of time, poor information, or great complexity typically found in most social situations yet omitted from the very simple situations postulated by most theorists militate against formation of minimal coalitions.[5]

Adrian and Press' "persuasion costs" are treated in some form by virtually every theorist. Every coalition member joins because he hopes to obtain payoff, policy goals, or other satisfactions. The concept of persuasion costs, then, is very general, and applies to any variable mentioned in any theory that accounts for participants' decisions to enter coalitions.

Vinacke (1959) raises a highly difficult problem for coalition theorists, the problem of participants' personality and motivations. He claims that some classes of participants respond to the emotional, rather than the payoff, aspects of coalition decisions. He produces experimental data to show that female subjects frequently eschew high payoffs in minimal coalitions in order to join less profitable coalitions with friends and thereby extends Gamson's hypothesis about non-utilitarian strategy preferences, saying that girls will prefer coalitions of friends even when they are in an inferior payoff class to other possible coalitions.

Vinacke's theory is hard to integrate into a dynamic theory of coalition formation, because it assumes that participants' personalities make them unable to respond to the objective aspects of the situation. If, however, Vinacke's assumptions are relaxed, to say that participants' non-payoff preferences (liking for particular persons, fear of competition, etc.) interact with payoff aspects of the situation, Vinacke's motivational variables can possibly explain some of the variance in coalition forming behavior.

B. Allocation of Payoffs

The distribution of rewards. As Gamson's (1964) review of the literature indicated, most theories—regardless of their underlying conceptual model—either predict or make firm assumptions about the distribution of rewards among members of the winning coalition. For the vast majority of theories, again regardless of their basic mode of explanation, predictions that rewards will be divided in some proportion to members' contribution of resources to the winning coalition are a necessary concomitant to predictions that winning coalitions will be minimal. If payoffs to individual members of a winning coalition are randomly assigned or bear no relationship to their contribution of resources, there is no reason for participants to concern themselves with attempts to control the sizes of winning coalitions.

For minimal coalition theories to hold, however, the relationship between resource contributions and payoffs need not be monotonic: Indeed as long as there is even an ordinal relationship between resources contributed and payoffs, there is reason for participants to form minimal winning coalitions.

The question of distribution of payoffs has received a great deal of logical and empirical analysis. Gamson (1966), for example, deals with the problem in terms of the concept of parity. He hypothesizes that members of the winning coalition share payoff strictly according to contributions of resources because of a belief that it is the only morally fair distribution scheme.

This rationale is supported by data from Gamson's experiments (1961b) and by transcripts of actual bargaining sessions in his and Riker's (1967) studies. But though the data support hypotheses based on the parity rationale, it is not clear that they confirm the moral belief logic. In fact, it might be argued that parity distributions of payoff can be explained more parsimoniously in two other ways: (1) in terms of Schelling's (1960) finding that people in bargaining situations can concert their behavior without communication, by letting the situation define "focal points". The contribution of resources is clearly a highly salient focal point in any bargaining among coalition members about payoff allocation; a related point (2) is consistent with Adrian and Press, that participants may allocate payoffs according to parity, not because they are persuaded by the moral arguments, but because following such an obvious scheme reduces bargaining costs.

However the parity hypothesis is founded, it must be stated only as an approximation of behavior. At least two careful experimenters have found that the distribution of payoffs is "flatter" than the distribution of resources within the winning coalition: though members with great resources receive higher payoffs than members with small resources, the former receive less and the latter more payoff than absolute parity would explain. Chertkoff's (1966) finding in this respect is especially interesting. In his study of situations in which no coalition was certain to win, he found that participants who contributed more than others to the chances for success received more payoff than others but less than their fully proportionate share. (This is also the prediction of Olson (1965) and Burgess and Robinson (1969) from the theory of public goods.)

Some theorists have proposed a very different explanation for distribution of payoffs. Shapley and Shubik (1954), predict that a coalition member's payoffs will be based on his pivotal power, i.e., the proportion of times his resources can change a losing proto-coalition into a winning one. Because this theory is operationally different from the parity hypothesis in only a special set of cases, it should be illustrated with a simple example.

In the case of a three member decision-making group where each member has identical resources, both the parity and pivotal power explanations make the same prediction: that two members will join a coalition and share payoffs equally. However, in a three member case where resources are distributed 2-1-2, the predictions vary. Parity-based theories would predict a 2-1 coalition, with the payoff distributed 66%-33%. The pivotal power rationale would predict that any two participants could join and share rewards equally.

The two rationales have received enough empirical support to suggest that both might be correct: the two processes might operate simultaneously in a given coalition situation. That, in fact, seems to be a good explanation for Chertkoff's findings and those of Kelley and Arrowood that the incidence of minimal coalitions with resources distributed according to parity decreases when a given decision-making group makes repeated decisions. This suggests that, as participants learn about bargaining with one another, they rely less on the anchoring points represented by a parity distribution, and gain more insight into the significance of pivotal power. As a matter of fact, the pivotal power concept makes sense only in repeated decisions, for in a one-time only decision, a participant's potential impact on other decisions is irrelevant. However, when participants expect to deal again with the same other persons, pivotal power becomes relevant, and it enters into the allocation of payoffs.

The lattice analysis research reviewed earlier (Brams and Riker (1970) and Brams and Heilman (1971)) introduces a new version of the parity hypothesis. It assumes that participants will act to maximize their expected share of spoils (ESS) from a winning coalition. ESS is a function of two variables: (1) the probability that the coalition which a participant joins will become winning in the future, and (2) the participant's own incremental contribution to that probability. As the lattice analysis shows, the values of these variables change as the coalition approaches winning size.

The basic hypothesis of their work is that a rational participant will join a coalition when his claim on the payoff—his ESS—is greatest. The validity of that hypothesis depends on the willingness of all members of the winning coalition to honor claims for payoff shares based on ESS.

The ESS concept is unique because it is based on the dynamics of the coalition forming process rather than on the initial distribution of resources.[6] But it requires the same assumption about ESS as the other parity theories do about resources, i.e., that the payoff allocation standard is compelling enough to convince even those coalition members who are relatively disadvantaged by it. That, like the other parity hypotheses, is an empirically verifiable proposition.

The hypothesis that winning coalition members will be rewarded on their ESS may, however, contain a contradiction. For the ESS hypothesis to hold, all participants must (1) understand that a member's incremental contribution to his coalition's winning depends on the time at which he joins the coalition, and (2) agree that the incremental contribution to the probability of winning should be the standard on which payoffs are allocated.

The contradiction is this: if all participants recognize the advantage of joining a coalition at the time at which ESS is highest, none would willingly join earlier or later than that time. Participants would be willing to join early or late only if they were promised compensating rewards. On the other hand, if only a few participants recognized the importance of ESS, the other coalition members would be unlikely to reward the sophisticated members on the basis of a standard they did not comprehend.

The resource-based parity hypothesis does not have these inconsistencies. Its strength is, as has been shown, that resources provide unambiguous standards on which to allocate rewards.

Exegesis of other works can uncover a few other implicit or partially developed hypotheses about distribution of payoff. Gamson (1964), for example, reviews two "theories" of coalition formation which would be inconsistent with either parity or pivotal power. Gamson's "anticompetitive theory" would certainly lead to the prediction of equal distribution of payoff among coalition members; his "utter confusion theory" leads to no particular prediction, although random or equal distribution of rewards payoffs would appear most likely.[7]

Although no researchers have deliberately incorporated bargaining skill as a variable in a theory, it could be the most important influence in a specific situation. Some reviews of the literature, including Gamson's, provide clues about why bargaining skill has not been treated. When participants expect the present decision-making group to make several future decisions, sharp bargaining can be dangerous. As Curry (1971) demonstrated, unreliable participants (sharp bargainers or seizers of the main chance) can elicit punitive reactions from the other participants. For this reason, it is very difficult to integrate bargaining skill into a theory: its precise operational definition would require measurement of others' responses, as well as of the skilled participants' behavior, and its operation in a specific case would depend on personality variables. For this reason, existing coalition theories might have inadvertently treated bargaining skill as well as it can be treated, by subsuming it under the parity concept. Indeed as pilot studies for this study and Schelling's work on interpersonal bargaining suggest, a participant who develops a reputation for fair play ultimately wins more than someone who bargains aggressively in the early going.

C. Tradeoffs Between Payoff and Non-Utilitarian Strategy Preferences

Until recently, few coalition theorists concerned themselves with situations in which the outcome of a coalition-forming decision could not be expressed on a single payoff dimension. The treatment of coalition outcomes as one-dimensional payoffs was a necessary simplification for the early development of coalition theory, but it has severely limited the applicability of coalition theories to natural political situations.

In most natural political situations, coalition formation affects more than the participants' personal payoffs. Decisions can affect participants' personal friendships, express or offend tastes, and, most importantly, affect the goods or privileges enjoyed by persons who are not members of the decision-making group.

Our introductory definitions called that last class of outcomes *policy*. In the natural political world most decision-making groups make policy as well as determine their members' personal payoffs.

One major goal of this study will be to explain the tradeoffs which participants make between payoffs and other outcomes, especially policy. For the moment, however, considerations of policy must be subsumed under a broader heading, i.e., nonutilitarian (nonpayoff) strategy preferences.

Gamson (1961a) introduced the concept of nonutilitarian strategy preferences. These preferences were for decisional outcomes other than payoff (his example was friendship where he predicted, and confirmed experimentally, that participants tend to prefer joining coalitions of friends over joining with strangers).

Gamson assigned nonutilitarian strategy preferences to a very weak position, hypothesizing that participants would exercise their nonpayoff preferences only when they could do it within a given payoff class. If one coalition satisfied nonutilitarian preferences more than another which offered the same payoff, the first would be chosen. However, according to Gamson's hypothesis, participants would not sacrifice any payoff to satisfy nonutilitarian strategy preferences.

Though Gamson's contribution was valuable, his assumption that payoff would always dominate other preferences was both unrealistic and unnecessary. The relative importance of payoff and other preferences can be expected to vary between participants and between situations. To integrate payoff and nonutilitarian considerations, a theory must admit the possibility that preferences for the two classes of outcomes might interact.

Leiserson (1970) tried to formulate a theory that recognized that payoff and nonutilitarian (specifically policy) might interact in determining coalition forming behavior.

Leiserson hypothesized that a participant would prefer the coalition which clearly satisfied one of his preferences: if a payoff-maximizing coalition could be formed readily, but one in which other members shared his policy views were difficult to obtain, the participant would opt for payoff-maximization, and vice-versa. In an ambiguous case, where neither preference was clearly the easier to satisfy, the participant would choose the coalition which maximized the expression

$$(r/R)W$$

where r = the participant's resources, R = the winning coalition's total resources, and W = the coalition's ideological worth (the nearness of the coalition's policy to the participant's own preferences.)

In a laboratory study, Leiserson generated data that supported his hypothesis: coalitions which clearly maximized one class of outcomes were preferred. When no clear maximizing strategy was available, the participants "traded off" between payoff and policy maximization. Leiserson interpreted this as support for his $(r/R)W$ expression.

Leiserson's work goes a long way toward establishing the proposition that participants' policy and payoff desires interact. However, some flaws in his methodology indicate just how primitive our understanding of policy-making is.

His expression $(r/R)W$ is really meant to be part of an equation which expressed in words is "the winning coalition will be the one which comes closest to jointly maximizing for all members the expressions (r/R) and W".

For any participant, the expression (r/R) is easy to compute for any possible coalition. The symbol W is easy to compute only if the observer knows in what units the participants measure ideological worth. Once it is measured, W can be integrated with (r/R) only if (1) they are measured in the same or comparable units or (2) each participant's relative preferences among units of (r/R) and W is known.

Leiserson avoided the problem neatly in his experiment. Winning coalition members' payoffs were measured in cash; subjects were assigned to hold ideological positions along a unidimensional scale; they were rewarded in cash for reducing the differences between their assigned position and the one adopted by the coalition.

The design did avoid the problems of measuring W and relating it to (r/R), but it did so by wholly confounding the two values. Because W adds to or subtracts from payoff directly, a strategy of jointly maximizing (r/R)W can readily be seen as merely maximizing payoff, without revealing anything about participants' tradeoffs between policy preferences and desires for payoff.

Axelrod (1967, 1969, 1971) has developed a concept of conflict of interest which will help express the extent to which a coalition is valuable in policy terms independent of its payoff value.

For any policy-making group whose members' policy preferences can be arrayed on a single dimension, conflict of interest can be conceptualized as the average distance between the preferred positions of two participants, when the maximum possible difference is standardized so as not to exceed 1.0. As Axelrod demonstrates, that proposition is equivalent to saying that the conflict of interest in any group is directly proportional to the variance of the distribution of the participants' policy preferences.

Axelrod bases a simple hypothesis on the conflict of interest concept: in political coalition situations in which policy is a relevant outcome, the coalition with the least conflict of interest (the one whose members' policy preferences have the smallest variance) is the most likely to form. This proposition can be related to participants' payoff preferences. By definition, coalitions with the least variance in policy preferences will have small numbers of members: once a coalition has enough members to win, the addition of any further members can only increase its policy variance. Likewise, the members of a least-variance coalition must be connected: no nonmember can hold a policy position between two members. Thus, Axelrod predicts that coalitions formed in policy situations will be minimal winning connected coalitions.

Axelrod's is a major contribution because it provides a way of expressing the policy value of a potential coalition—in terms of the variance of the members' preferences. The policy value of a coalition can be expressed as the inverse of the variance of members' policy preferences.

Axelrod's formulation is wholly satisfactory for situations in which all participants have equal resources, but it does not make clear predictions when winning coalitions with equal numbers of members have unequal resources. In those situations, where participants must trade off between policy satisfaction and payoff, his minimal connected winning coalition hypothesis cannot explain the outcome.

Hence, theory which places payoff and policy satisfaction in a fully dynamic relationship—one that explains the tradeoffs that participants make between payoff and policy outcomes—remains to be developed. Axelrod's conceptualization of conflict of interest will be useful in the next chapter, which tries to develop such a theory.

A final contribution to this element of the literature was made by Adrian and Press (1968). In their discussion of decision costs, they identify two which have some impact on policy. "Dissonance costs" are functions of the degree to which potential members of the minimum winning coalition disagree about a policy which they must make. "Responsibility costs" are functions of the degree to which a policy adversely affects persons who are not members of the decision-making group. In short, the lower the dissonance costs the more likely the formation of a minimum winning coalition.

Operationally, that hypothesis is very much like Leiserson's prediction that the chosen coalition will be the one which maximizes the expression $(r/R)W$. It expresses the insight that payoffs and policy considerations jointly affect the choice of a coalition (or that the chosen policy is a joint effect of the coalition members' relative weight and the distribution of policy preferences among the members.) It does not specify the manner in which policy differences can be quantified, thereby avoiding question of the interaction between the two elements of the $(r/R)W$ expression.

In general, hypotheses about policy-making have recognized that payoff and policy variables are related, but they have not made quantitative statements about that relationship. The reason is clear: no neat theories exist that will predict the relationship a priori. To measure the relationship between payoff considerations and policy desires, it will be necessary to set the variables at work empirically, and to assess their interactions carefully.

CONCLUSION

This review has considered the common and unique contributions of coalition theories from three major research traditions. The review demonstrates that the three approaches produce theories which approach certain common problems in basically similar ways. It shows that many of the most valuable insights of the various coalition theories can be stated consistently and with equal validity in terms of more than one model. This suggests—as the review set out to establish—that there are grounds for an effort to synthesize the common and unique insights of existing theories into one comprehensive theory. That will be the work of the next section.

III. A THEORY OF POLITICAL COALITIONS IN SIMPLE AND POLICY SITUATIONS

The preceeding review has laid out the details of existing coalition theories in considerable detail. It identified a number of variables which affect various aspects of coalition formation. But it did not show how the diverse insights of existing theories can be integrated into a single theory, nor did it demonstrate how a single theory can explain coalition formation in the whole range of situations which coalition theory addresses.

The review did show that the theories share many insights, and that many of the concepts can be reformulated in terms consistent with the structures of any of the three basic models. On the other hand, the social-psychological model appears to be the broadest, most versatile, simplest to operationalize, and consequently the most appropriate for a synthesis of the existing theories. Therefore, the purpose of this section will be to use the social-psychological model to produce a single theory which integrates the basic insights of the existing theories.

Before stating the theory, we must define its basic unit of analysis, its assumptions, the phenomena which its tries to explain.

LEVEL OF ANALYSIS AND ASSUMPTIONS

The basic unit of analysis for this theory is the individual actor. To use the individual participant as the basic unit of analysis requires several assumptions:

(1) The an actor's perceptions of a situation determine his behavior;

(2) That actors place themselves in the coalition situation to obtain the benefits which the situation uniquely provides. This means that the "objective" outcomes of the coalition decision—payoff in a simple coalition situation, and both payoff and non-utilitarian outcomes in a multidimensional outcome situation—are of primary interest for the participant.

(3) That participants prefer obtaining more rather than less of the benefits which the situation provides and will consequently prefer coalitions which promise greater rather than lesser benefits.

Based on these assumptions, the theory will predict the participant's choices of coalition partners. It will not, at least in the beginning, predict mutual choices among participants. Ultimately, mutual choices determine which coalitions will be formed. But mutual choices are merely summations of individual choices and individual choices are causally prior to mutual choices. When initial choices are not reciprocated, participants must seek reciprocity with their secondary preferences, and so on. Ultimately, the theory must explore those secondary preferences. But initial preferences are most indicative of the causes of coalition formation, and must be explored first.

Specification of Dependent Variables. As Chapter One indicated, the theory will explain three dependent variables, each an aspect of the individual participant's choice of winning coalition partners. They are: (1) the total resources of the chosen winning coalition, (2) the degree to which payoffs are allocated according to resource-parity, and (3) the satisfaction of the participant's non-utilitarian strategy preferences.

(1) Total resources of the chosen winning coalition: explanation of the size of winning coalitions is the prime historic concern of political coalition theory. Consistent with that tradition, this theory will concentrate first on explaining the total resources of the chosen winning coalition. That dependent variable will be designated by the symbol R. In any given coalition situation the range of values of R is determined by the difference between the total resources of the minimum winning coalition and the coalition of the whole. Thus, any independent variable that makes a participant likely to choose a minimum winning coalition can be said, on the average, to decrease the value of R. Conversely, variables which make the participant unlikely to choose a minimum winning coalition can be said, on the average, to increase the value of R.

(2) Allocation of payoffs. In the literature, the discussion of allocations of payoffs is generally analogous to the treatment of coalition size: theories identify independent variables which increase or decrease the likelihood that payoffs will be allocated according to the resource parity standard. This theory will follow suit, by explaining the deviations of the allocations of payoffs from the resource parity standard.

(3) Satisfaction of nonutilitarian strategy preferences. No theory except Axelrod's (1971) has defined the non-payoff outcomes of coalition formation in such a way as to permit operational definition. The reason, of course, is that the number and variety of such preferences is virtually infinite: it can include friendship, convenience, constituency interests, ideology, and many others.

One class of nonutilitarian strategy preferences does stand out as being uniquely interesting to political scientists. That is the class of preferences which operate when a winning coalition makes policy as well as allocates payoffs among its members.[8] This theory will explain the satisfaction of policy preferences in coalition decisions.

Any participant who is not completely indifferent about the policy issue being decided will choose the coalition that will make the policy most consistent with his preferences. For the participant, the degree to which the coalition he chooses is composed of others who share his preferences will determine his policy satisfaction. Policy satisfaction, the third dependent variable of the new theory, is a function of the distribution of policy preferences in the participant's chosen winning coalition. It varies inversely with the deviation of other winning coalition members' preferences from the participant's own preference.

These assumptions and definitions lead to the exposition of the theory. For the sake of clarity, the exposition will proceed in three stages. Part One states the theory in its most elementary form, as it applies to situations whose only outcomes are the participants' payoffs, i.e., simple coalition situations. Part Two extends the theory to situations in which winning coalitions make policy in addition to allocating payoffs among winning coalition members. Part Three integrates the propositions of parts one and two into a full statement of the theory.

PART 1.
SIMPLE COALITION SITUATIONS

Simple coalition situations—those whose only outcome is the allocation of payoffs among members of the winning coalition—probably exist only in the minds and laboratories of theorists. Because payoff is the only possible outcome, choices of coalition partners in simple situations can be explained entirely in terms of participants' efforts to obtain payoffs for themselves.

A basic insight of the entire theory is the minimum winning coalition hypothesis: since every participant prefers a greater payoff to a lesser one, and since payoffs must be divided among members of the winning coalition, then any participant will choose to maximize his own payoff by keeping the number of competing claims to an absolute minimum. The most direct way for the participant to minimize others' claims on payoff is to choose a winning coalition in which the ratio of his own resources to total coalition resources is the highest possible. If the participant's resources are r, and total coalition resources are R, the winning coalition in which r/R has the highest possible value is the one in which R has the lowest possible value.[9]

That, by definition, is the minimum winning coalition.

The connection between choosing a minimum winning coalition and receiving the maximum possible payoff can be understood by anyone who can compute a ratio.

However, a number of variables can clarify or obscure that relationship, and thus increase or decrease the likelihood that the participant will choose a minimum winning coalition. The remainder of this section identifies those variables and explains the dynamics by which they affect a participant's choice of coalition partners.

Variables that clarify or obscure relationships between minimum winning coalitions and maximum payoffs fall into five classes: (1) information, (2) complexity, (3) assurance of parity allocation of payoff, (4) continuity of the decision-making group, and (5) uncertainty about the difference between controlling and winning coalitions. For the remainder of Part One the exposition of the theory will be organized around these five classes of independent variables.

(1) Information. When a participant lacks complete information about the coalition situation—about its decision-making rules or about his and others' resources—the relationship between a minimal winning coalition and maximum payoff becomes obscure. Without firm information about decision-making rules, the participant cannot know what level of resources are minimally required to win. Likewise, incomplete information about his and others' resources destroys a participant's ability to identify the members of a minimal winning coalition.

According to assumption 3 (above) a participant prefers winning something to winning nothing at all. When he is uncertain about how the game is played or who has what resources, the participant will choose a coalition which he thinks will give him a "margin of safety"—i.e., he will deliberately choose a coalition that he thinks is somewhat larger than the minimal winning size.

The degree to which the participant will deliberately "hedge" against uncertainty depends on the amount of information which he has. When he has little or no information the participant will choose the largest coalition he can, in hopes of winning at least something. When his information is nearly complete, the participant will choose a coalition which offers only a small margin of safety.

Thus, information affects the size of participant's chosen winning coalitions inversely: as the completeness of information increases the total resources of the chosen winning coalition (R) decrease.

(2) Complexity. When the participant is unable to comprehend the coalition situation because he has too much information to integrate in the time available to him, he endures uncertainties analogous to those he

would face in a situation of inadequate information. Both too little and too much information force the participant to construct margins of safety in forming winning coalitions.

Thus, complexity affects the size of winning coalitions directly. As complexity increases R increases.

(3) Assurance of parity allocation of payoffs. As Gamson (1961a), Riker (1962b), and others have noted, for participants to choose coalitions according to the minimum winning coalition hypothesis, they must have some reason to assume that their payoffs will reflect their contribution of resources to the winning coalition. A participant who does not expect his payoff to be affected by the ratio of his resources to those of the entire winning coalition will have little reason to choose a minimal winning coalition.

A critical factor making total coalition resources salient is the assurance that payoffs will indeed be allocated among coalition members according to their relative contributions of resources to the winning coalition. The degree to which the winning coalition's payoffs will be allocated according to resource-parity will affect the participant's choice of coalition partners. As the assurance of parity allocation increases, and as the linkage between minimum winning coalitions and maximum payoffs becomes apparent, R decreases. Conversely, as assurance of parity allocation decreases, the linkage between minimum winning coalitions and maximum personal payoffs becomes obscure. Thus, as parity assurance decreases, R increases.

(4) Continuity of the decision-making group. It is possible for an actor to be certain about which is a minimal winning coalition in a single decision without being able to determine which coalition will bring him the greatest ultimate payoff. This applies particularly to situations in which the decision-making group is continuous. When a group persists over several decisions (for example, a Congressional committee) a participant will consider the implications of his present actions for his prospects of repeating as a member of future winning coalitions, and this consideration should lead the participant to choose larger-than-minimal winning coalitions for two reasons. First, a participant can have greater assurance of winning in the long term if he chooses a winning coalition which can persist over several decisions rather than a coalition which can win in only one decision. This can be achieved by choosing a larger-than-minimal coalition, which can win in the future even if it loses some members.

Second, as Curry (1971) has suggested, members can expect that participants excluded from payoff in the present decision are likely to be hard bargainers in future decisions. If the present winning coalition is likely to lose members in the future, the participant must anticipate the need to form coalitions with others who might be deprived of payoff if a minimal coalition were formed in the present case. Choosing a larger-than-minimal coalition in the present decision assures the participant of a large pool of friendly potential partners for future decisions.

Thus, for the sake of security in future decisions, a participant in a continuous decision-making group will choose a coalition larger than necessary to win in a single instance. To some degree, the total resources of chosen coalitions will depend on the number of decisions to be made: a participant expecting the decision-making group to last through two or three decisions will probably not need as great a margin of safety as one who must anticipate fifty or more future decisions. Though the total resources of a chosen coalition can be expected to increase as a function of the number of anticipated decisions, that function cannot be described a priori—nor is it possible at this time to specify the limit at which chosen coalition reaches its maximum size. For the present the proposition that R increases as the continuity of the decision-making group increases must suffice.

Some coalition theories have linked the continuity of the decision-making group to another dependent variable. Chertkoff (1966) and Kelley and Arrowood (1960) have shown that the continuity of the decision-making group affects the allocation of payoffs among participants. That relationship can illuminate some aspects of participants' choices of partners in simple coalition situations, and should be treated here.

In a terminal coalition situation payoff allocation is straightforward. Participants who are potential members of a minimal winning coalition will see that the unique benefit of membership in a winning coalition depends on each member's obtaining payoff in proportion to his contribution of resources. Without any need to consider future decisions, a minimal winning coalition with payoffs allocated in proportion to resources is more attractive than larger coalitions or coalitions with unknown standards for allocating payoffs.

But when a decision-making group is continuous (i.e., makes many successive decisions) resources lose their utility as a base for estimating payoff shares. As the argument above implies, participants who would be excluded from a minimal winning coalition in a single decision are likely to be included in at least some of the winning coalitions of a continuing decision-making group.

Participants whose resources exclude them from membership in a minimal winning coalition (e.g., the actor whose resources are 50 in a decision-making group where resources are distributed 30-21-50) must either accept continual losing or become willing to accept payoffs lower than their proportionate contribution of resources. Thus, participants whose resources are too great to permit them to become members of minimal coalitions will accept less than their proportionate payoffs. Their most likely strategy is to offer disproportionately large payoffs to minimal coalition members who have small resources. Participants who would receive high payoffs in minimal coalitions can counter that strategy only by accepting disproportionately small payoffs. As a result, participants' expectations for payoffs will become "flatter" (e.g., closer to absolute equality) than the distribution of resources.

This process is not instantaneous: participants must either have time to analyze the likely moves and countermoves in advance or, more likely, experience the gradual flattening of payoff demands over several decisions.

Thus, multiple decisions complicate the measurement of resources. A participant's resources in a single decision become confounded with the likelihood of his becoming a winning coalition member in future decisions. Ultimately, the problem of becoming a member of the winning coalition becomes more important than obtaining payoffs commensurate with resources.

This argument has important consequences for two dependent variables, (1) the allocation of payoffs among winning coalition members, and (2) R, the total resources of the chosen winning coalition.

As the number of decisions to be made increases, the allocation of payoffs among winning coalition members diverges from resource parity, and increasingly resembles absolute equality. As the relationship between winning coalition members' resources and the allocation of payoffs weakens, a participant is less and less likely to chose a minimal winning coalition.

The continuity of the decision-making group is related to R in two ways: First, it increases it directly, by encouraging participants to build winning coalitions which have "margins of safety" for future decisions. Second, it increases R indirectly, by weakening the relationship between participants' resources and their payoffs (i.e., decreasing parity in the allocation of payoffs), and thus discouraging the participant from expecting a maximum payoff from the minimum winning coalition.

(5) A distinction between *controlling* and *winning* coalitions. A special case of inadequate information occurs when a coalition large enough to control the decision-making group may not be able to obtain payoffs to allocate among members. Participants in nominating conventions and legislative committees often face the distinction between controlling and winning coalitions.

A participant's behavior will depend on whether there are benefits from controlling that are independent of the benefits from winning. If benefits can be obtained only by winning, a participant will choose a coalition with the resources to win over a coalition which only has the resources to control the decision-making group. If the resources needed to win are of a different nature than the resources needed to control (e.g., national popularity vs. seniority in the party) the participant will choose a coalition with the resources required to win. As the certainty with which the participant can identify the minimal winning coalition increases, R decreases.

If the participant can identify potential controlling coalitions but does not know which coalition can win, he must rely on the best indicator he has of the resources required to win. That indicator is the resources required to control. Using that indicator, the coalition with the most of the resources required to control appears to be the one with the best chance of winning. Thus, in situations where a participant cannot identify any sure winning coalition, he will choose the largest controlling coalition he can aggregate. As the difficulty in distinguishing controlling from winning coalitions increases, R increases.

Figure 1, below, presents an efficient summary of the theory for simple coalition situations. It indicates the nature of the relationship between each independent variable and the dependent variable, R (total resources of the chosen coalition). It also illustrates the status of the variable "parity allocation of payoffs" as an intervening (partly dependent and partly independent) variable in the theory.

PART 2
POLICY COALITION SITUATIONS

Part One dealt with coalition situations whose only outcomes are the participants' payoffs. This part deals with a far more realistic set of situations, those in which the formation of a winning coalition has other consequences in addition to the participants' payoff. Though an infinite number of such nonpayoff outcomes are possible, this discussion will concentrate on the one which is of most direct concern to political science, namely the making of policy.

As the remainder of this section will demonstrate, the theory to explain coalition formation in policy situations builds on the theory for simple situations.[10] The theory becomes more elaborate without contradicting any of the propositions of Part 1.

Because the theory for policy situations involves many simultaneous

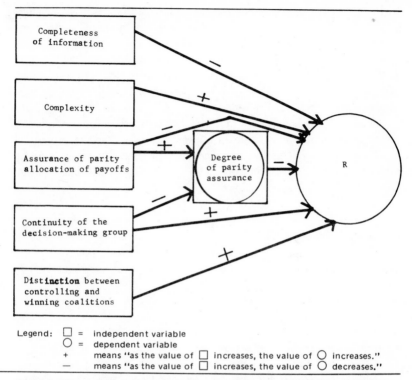

Figure 1: Determinants of the Total Resources (R) of the Chosen Winning Coalition in Simple Situations.

relationship, it is best expressed as a mathematical model. The elements of the model are: (1) the payoff available to the participant, (2) the policy satisfaction available to the participant, (3) the intensity of the participant's desire for payoff, and (4) the intensity of the participant's desire for policy satisfaction. The following discussion develops techniques for expressing the elements of the model and derives theoretical propositions from them.

Payoff, the only outcome of decisions in simple coalition situations, is an important element of the model for policy situations. For a member of the winning coalition, it can be expressed by: $A (r/R)$, where A = total payoff for the winning coalition. [11] (r/R) = the ratio of the participant's resources to the total resources of the winning coalition.

The concept of policy satisfaction is a new one. It involves two variables: (1) the participant's policy position and (2) potential coalition partners' policy positions.

Axelrod's "conflict of interest" concept and his hypothesis that participants are most satisfied with—and therefore most willing to join—a coalition whose members' policy preferences have the least mutual variance are relevant here. Assuming that coalitions will take policy positions that reflect the central tendency of their members' preferences, an individual participant will expect to derive the most policy satisfaction from the coalition whose members' preferences differ least from his own. In operational terms, a participant will derive the greatest policy satisfaction from the coalition whose "central tendency" on policy most closely corresponds to his own preference.[12]

Adapting the conflict of interest concept, we can say that a participant's policy satisfaction in a given coalition decreases monotonically with any increases in the variance of the other coalition members' positions around his own position. If the variance around his own position is expressed as

$$\frac{\Sigma(X_i-X_p)^2}{N}$$

where X_p is the participant's own position, X_i represents the positions of all other members of the coalition, and N is the number of members of the coalition, then the participant's policy satisfaction can be estimated[13] as

$$\frac{1}{\frac{\Sigma(X_i-X_p)^2}{N}}$$

That expression has one serious flaw: a coalition among participants who share an identical policy preference will result in an infinite satisfaction value (1/0). This can be corrected by normalizing satisfaction to a value of 1, thus: satisfaction can be estimated as some monotone function of the value of the expression

$$\frac{1}{1 + \frac{\Sigma(X_i-X_p)^2}{N}}$$

(For convenience, policy satisfaction will hereafter be PS.)

The absolute value of this satisfaction expression will depend partly on the scale on which policy preferences are measures. A 10-point scale will produce higher satisfaction values than a 100-point scale, simply because the absolute value of the variance will be lower. But the size of the scale used to measure policy differences will not affect the relative scores of alternative coalitions in a given situation.

For some policy situations, the elements of the model now developed would suffice to explain a participant's choice of a coalition. Whenever it is possible for a participant to choose a single coalition that maximizes both his payoff (A r/R) and his policy satisfaction (PS)

$$\frac{1}{1 + \dfrac{\Sigma(X_i - X_p)^2}{N}}$$

the prediction of his choice is a simple exercise. He will choose the coalition that maximizes either (and thus by definition both) his payoff and his PS.

Though that prediction is a simple one, it is not as trivial as it may sound: as Axelrod (1969, 1971) and Adrian and Press (1968) have both demonstrated, policy situations in which all participants have equal resources always have at least one coalition which maximizes both payoff and PS simultaneously.[14]

However, the model is of special importance when no one coalition will maximize both payoff and PS for the participant. This can happen readily when participants have unequal resources. In that case, the participant must accept some tradeoff between payoff and PS. For the model to predict and explain those tradeoffs, it must be enlarged to include some expressions of the participant's readiness to trade off between payoff and PS. Those expressions will represent the participant's intensities of preference for payoff and policy satisfactions, respectively. As an expression of the relative strengths of the participant's payoff and policy preferences, intensity can permit us to estimate the rate at which the participant will trade off units of PS for units of payoff. Though the concept does present measurement problems it is conceptually possible to measure the two preferences on identical scales.

The intensity concept has two elements: the strength of the participant's preference for payoff (I_p) and the strength of his preference for policy satisfaction (I_s). Intensity can be expressed as a pure number (the ratio of I_s to I_p) and used to adjust the policy satisfaction expression so its value is comparable to the payoff term. Or I_p and I_s can be used separately as coefficients to adjust then respective expressions.

Choosing the latter technique, we can construct an expression which resolves the payoff and PS available to the participant to a single value. The expression will have an exact value for every possible coalition. The coalition chosen (C_i) will be the one whose value in the expression is the greatest. Thus, every other coalition $C_{j...n}$ will have a value for the following expression which is less than that for C_i:

$$(A\,r/R) \cdot I_p + \left[\left(\frac{1}{1 + \dfrac{\Sigma(X_i - X_p)^2}{N}}\right)\right] \cdot I_s$$

where A = the total payoff available to the winning coalition, r = the participant's own resources, R = total resources of the coalition,

r/R = ratio of the participant's resources to the total resources of the coalition, and I_p and I_s = participant's intensities of preference for payoff and policy satisfaction, respectively

$$\cfrac{1}{1 + \cfrac{\Sigma(X_i - X_p)^2}{N}}$$

= an estimate of the policy satisfaction (PS) that what the participant derives from membership in the coalition.

In any coalition situation, finding C_i is a matter of filling in the values of the expression. Once C_i is identified the dependent variables of interest can be observed directly.

The model applies as well to situations in which a single coalition maximizes both payoff and PS as to situations in which the participant must trade off between the two outcomes.

However, the model has surprisingly different implications in tradeoff situations than in situations in which the two outcomes can be maximized by a single coalition.

To illustrate the ways in which the model differentiates between situations, let us extract the model's consequences for the two kinds of situations.

First, situations in which both payoff and policy satisfaction can be maximized jointly. By definition $(A\ r/R)$ increases as

$$\cfrac{1}{1 + \cfrac{\Sigma(X_i - X_p)^2}{N}}$$

increases.

If the participant chooses a coalition with a high r/R ratio, he automatically chooses one with high PS, and vice-versa. If the participant's I_s is high, he chooses the coalition which offers the highest PS; in doing so, he will also maximize his $(A\ r/R)$ value.

In tradeoff situations the relationships are far more complex. By definition, any factor that causes a participant to choose to maximize one outcome causes him also to sacrifice some of the other outcome.

Thus, a participant with a high I_p is likely to choose a coalition which would provide him a large payoff. That choice would be for a coalition low in total resources and also low in policy satisfaction. Conversely, a participant with a high I_s is likely to choose a coalition which would provide him high policy satisfaction. That coalition would necessarily have a higher-than-minimal R, and thus less than the maximum payoff.

A participant in a situation in which the winning coalition's total payoff, (A), is very high would be likely to choose a coalition which gives him a high proportion of the payoff. That coalition would necessarily have a low R, and provide lower PS than other possible coalitions. Conversely, a participant in a situation in which one coalition offered very high PS would be likely to choose that coalition. That coalition would necessarily have a high R, and thus provide him less payoff than other possible coalitions.

Figure 2 illustrates the manner in which the model's properties differ between joint maximizing and tradeoff situations.

PART 3
INTEGRATION

Parts 1 and 2 both identify variables that explain participants' choices of winning coalitions. Both parts explain R, total resources of the chosen coalition, albeit under different special conditions. But, as an inspection of

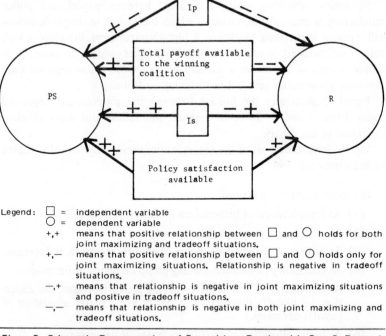

Legend: □ = independent variable
O = dependent variable
+,+   means that positive relationship between □ and O holds for both joint maximizing and tradeoff situations.
+,—   means that positive relationship between □ and O holds only for joint maximizing situations. Relationship is negative in tradeoff situations.
—,+   means that relationship is negative in joint maximizing situations and positive in tradeoff situations.
—,—   means that relationship is negative in both joint maximizing and tradeoff situations.

Figure 2: Schematic Representation of Propositions Developed in Part 2: Determinants of the Total Resources (R) of the Chosen Coalition and of the Participant's Policy Satisfaction (PS) from His Chosen Coalition, in Policy-Making Situations.

Figures 1 and 2 reveals, the variables affecting R in simple situations have not been related to variables affecting R in policy situations.

The purpose of this short Part is to integrate Parts 1 and 2. The integration can be achieved directly: the policy situation model has nothing to contribute to the explanation of participants' choices of coalitions in simple situations; but any factor that affects R in a simple situation will have a similar effect in a policy situation. Completeness of information and assurance of parity allocation of payoff both decrease R while complexity and a distinction between controlling and winning coalitions both increase R.

In situations which do not require tradeoffs between payoff and policy satisfaction, the participant will choose coalitions with a low R, even despite complexity, low information, continuity of the decision-making group, or a difference between controlling and winning coalitions. But that will be due to those coalitions' high policy satisfaction, not because of their low R.

In policy situations where a tradeoff between payoff and policy satisfaction is unavoidable, variables which increase R in simple situations will cause a participant to choose a high-resource (and therefore a high policy satisfaction) winning coalition. Variables which decrease R in simple situations will cause a participant to choose a low resource (and therefore a low policy satisfaction) winning coalition.

Figure 3 illustrates the linkage between the propositions expressed under Parts 1 and 3. It is, in a sense, the fullest and most efficient statement of the theory.

Figure 3 represents all of the theory's hypotheses schematically. Stated verbally they are:

In simple coalition situations,

(1) As completeness of information increases, R decreases.

(2) As complexity increases, R increases.

(3) As assurance of parity allocation of payoffs increases, R decreases.

(4) As continuity of decision-making group increases, R increases.

(5) As continuity of the decision-making group increases, the allocation of payoffs diverges from parity (i.e., parity allocation of payoffs decreases.)

(6) As parity allocation of payoffs increases, R decreases.

(7) As the distinction between controlling and winning coalitions increases, R increases.

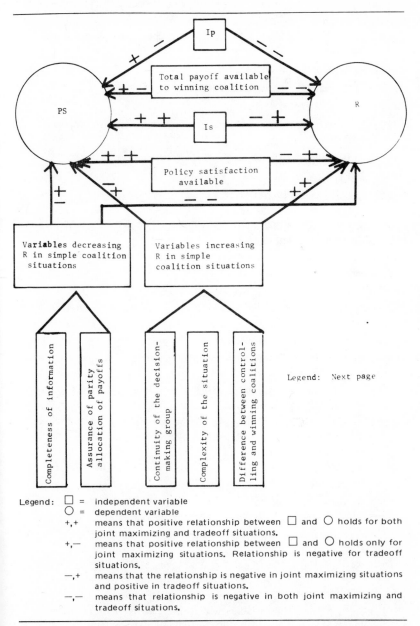

Legend: □ = independent variable
○ = dependent variable
+,+ means that positive relationship between □ and ○ holds for both joint maximizing and tradeoff situations.
+,— means that positive relationship between □ and ○ holds only for joint maximizing situations. Relationship is negative for tradeoff situations.
—,+ means that the relationship is negative in joint maximizing situations and positive in tradeoff situations.
—,— means that relationship is negative in both joint maximizing and tradeoff situations.

Figure 3: Complete Statement of the Determinants of the Total Resources (R) of the Chosen Coalition and the Participant's Policy Satisfaction (PS) from His Chosen Coalition, in Policy-Making Situations.

In policy coalition situations in which payoff and policy satisfaction (PS) can be maximized jointly,

  (8) As total payoff available to the winning coalition increases, R decreases.

  (9) As I_p increases, R decreases.

  (10) As PS available increases, R decreases.

  (11) As I_s increases, R decreases.

  (12) As total payoff available to the winning coalition increases, PS increases.

  (13) As I_p increases, PS increases.

  (14) As PS available increases, PS increases.

  (15) As I_s increases, PS increases.

In policy coalition situations in which payoff and policy satisfaction (PS) cannot be maximized jointly,

  (16) As total payoff available to the winning coalition increases, R decreases.

  (17) As the participant's I_p increases, R decreases.

  (18) As the amount of PS available to the participant increases, R increases.

  (19) As the participant's I_s increases, R increases.

  (20) As the values of variables which increase R in simple situations increase, R increases.

  (21) As the values of variables which decrease R in simple situations increase, R decreases.

  (22) As the total payoff available to the winning coalition increases, the PS which the participant derives from his chosen coalition decreases.

  (23) As the participant's I_p increases, the PS which he derives from his chosen coalition decreases.

  (24) As the amount of PS available to the participant increases, the PS which he derives from his chosen coalition increases.

  (25) As the participant's I_s increases, the PS which he derives from his chosen coalition increases.

  (26) As the values of variables which increase R in simple situations increase, the PS which the participant derives from his chosen coalition increases.

  (27) As the values of variables which decrease R in simple situations increase, the PS which the participant derives from his chosen coalition decreases.

SUMMARY AND CONCLUSION

This paper has synthesized the central propositions of some diverse coalition theories into a single internally-consistent theory of coalition formation. It then extended coalition theory's explanatory power into an area which had previously been treated cursorily or ignored, namely situations in which winning coalitions make policy as well as allocate payoffs among participants.

The theory stated here is incomplete in many respects. Many of the independent variables are generic only: the theory could gain explanatory power if some of those variables (e.g., complexity) were defined more exactly in terms of specific operating characteristics of coalition situations.

At this point, the key to improvement of the theory is empirical—probably experimental—work which operationalizes the independent variables, tests the effects of each, and observes all the independent variables acting simultaneously under controlled conditions.

NOTES

1. Curry (1971) makes the useful point that the coalition pattern of interaction can be adopted only if the participants choose to do so. In some situations, as Curry demonstrated, the coalition pattern is relatively unlikely to develop. Situations are political to the degree that the coalition pattern is likely because (a) the situation offers no rewards whatever for the single participant, and (b) the rewards for members of a group that is large enough to win but smaller than the whole are greater than the rewards for members of a coalition of the whole.

The definition is context-free, in that it identifies situations as political according to their operating characteristics rather than by their relationships to specific institutions or arenas. Other theorists writing outside formal coalition literature (including Easton (1953), Lasswell (1962), and Morgenthau (1961)), have advanced similarly general definitions of the political. As Easton notes (1953), focusing attention to the common dynamics of such diverse arenas as political conventions, tribal councils, and church synods is as essential to the building of general theory as it is inessential to simple institutional description.

2. Hence, (payoff = (winners' reward − losers' rewards). Where losers' reward = 0, payoff = winners' reward).

3. It is not altogether clear whether Riker wishes to assume cognitive mediation between the situation's mathematical properties and participant's forming minimal coalitions: in a recent article, for example, Riker (1967) notes that some of his experimental subjects made the cognitive linkage, but claims that the mathematical properties "control" behavior whether they are recognized or not.

4. Gamson's and Leiserson's contributions will be discussed in detail in the section about policy as a dependent variable.

5. Adrian and Press' work suggests that simplicity-complexity is a continuum, rather than a dichotomy. The effects of complexity on the size and character of a winning coalition can and should be measured, rather than ignored through simplifying assumptions and postulates.

6. The authors do not reject the resource-parity concept. They simply ignore it for analytical convenience by assuming that all participants have equal weight. Unequal resources would complicate the calculation of ESS, but they could be incorporated.

7. Anticompetitive theory rests on the assumption that all actors wish to avoid conflict more than they desire the rewards of coalitional decisions. Thus, it predicts that rewards will be shared equally among all actors. Utter confusion theory assumes that most decisions are too complex for actors to understand. Thus, the distribution of rewards is random and on the average equal among all actors.

8. For the definition of policy see Section 1, page 8.

9. For simplicity the dependent variable "total resources of the chosen winning coalition" will be symbolized by R. In any coalition situation, R will be at its lowest value in the minimal winning coalition and at its highest value in he coalition of the whole. An independent variable which contributes to the choice of the minimal winning coalition will be said to decrease R; a variable which makes the choice of a larger-than-minimal winning coalition likely will be said to increase R.

The following illustrate these procedures graphically.

"As X_i increases, R increases."

X_i

"As X_j increases, R decreases."

X_j

10. Definitions of "simple" and "policy" situations are presented in Section 1, page 8.

11. Because this theory treats only constant sum situations, A is the same for all possible winning coalitions in a given situation.

12. Two recent contributions to the literature of coalition theory employ the central tendency assumption. James P. Zais and John H. Kessel (1970) assume that the attitudinal position of a coalition is best represented by its "center of gravity", which in their simulation was a mean position weighted by the importance of different coalition members. Abraham DeSwaan (1970) assumes that the policy preference of the member holding the median position is the best estimate of the coalition's final position.

13. Whether the real policy satisfaction function is linear must be determined empirically. At this point, we can only estimate it by assuming linearity.

14. As Axelrod (1969) has shown, the least-variance concept of policy satisfaction implies that the chosen coalition will have the smallest possible number of members. But in cases where participants have unequal resources, the coalition with the highest policy satisfaction score might not be the one with minimal resources. In such cases the participant must trade off between payoff and policy satisfaction.

REFERENCES

ADRIAN, C. R. and C. PRESS (1968) "Decision costs in coalition formation." American Political Science Rev. 62: 556-564.

AXELROD, R. (1971) Conflict of Interest. New York: Markham.

––– Derivation of a Coalition Theory Based on Conflict of Interest with an application to Italy. Paper delivered to the 1969 Convention of American Political Science Association.

––– (1967) "Conflict of interest, an axiomatic approach." Journal of Conflict Resolution 11: 86-99.

BRAMS, S. J. and W. H. RIKER. Models of Coalition Formation in Voting Bodies. Paper delivered to the 1970 Convention of the American Political Association.

BRAMS, S. J. and J. G. HEILMAN. When to Join a Coalition, and with How Many Others, Depends on What you Expect the Outcome to be. Paper delivered. to the 1971 Convention of the American Political Science Association.

BURGESS, P. M. and J. A. ROBINSON (1969) "Alliances and the theory of collective action: a simulation of coalition processes." Midwest Journal of Political Science 12: 194-218.

CHERTKOFF, J. M. (1970) "Sociopsychological theories and research on coalition formation," in Groenings, Sven et al. (eds.) The Study of Coalition Behavior. New York: Holt, Rinehart and Winston.

––– (1960) "The effects of probability of future success on coalition formation." Journal of Experimental Social Psychology 2: 265-277.

CURRY, T. J. Toward a New Theory of Coalition Formation. Unpublished Ph.D. dissertation, University of Washington, 1971.

DeSWAAN, A. (1970) "An empirical model of coalition formation as an N-Person game of policy distance minimization," in Groenings (ed.) Coalition Behavior, 425-444.

EASTON, D. (1953) The Political System. New York: Knopf.

GAMSON, W. A. (1964) "Experimental studies of coalition formation," in L. Berkowitz (ed.) Advances in Experimental Social Psychology 1: 81-110.

––– (1961a) "A theory of coalition formation." American Sociological Rev. 26: 373-382.

––– (1961b) "An experimental test of a theory of coalition formation." American Sociological Rev. 26: 565-573.

HOFFMAN, P. J., L. FESTINGER, and D. H. LAWRENCE (1954) "Tendencies toward group comparability in competitive bargaining." Human Relations 1: 141-157.

KELLEY, E. W. (1968) "Techniques of studying coalition formation." Midwest Journal of Political Science 12: 26-84.

KELLEY, H. H. and A. J. ARROWOOD (1960) "Coalitions in the triad: critique and experiment." Sociometry 23: 231-244.

LASSWELL, H. (1962) The Future of Political Science. London: Tavistock.

LEISERSON, M. (1970) "Power and ideology in coalition behavior," in Groenings (ed.) Coalition Behavior.

––– (1968) "Factions and coalitions in one-party Japan." American Political Science Rev. 62: 770-787.

MORGENTHAU, H. J. (1961) Politics Among Nations. New York: Knopf.

OLSON, M., Jr. (1965) The Logic of Collective Action. Cambridge: Harvard Univ. Press.

RIKER, W. H. (1967) "Bargaining in a three-person game." American Political Scienve Rev. 61: 642-656.

——— (1962a) "A new proof of the size principle," in J. L. Bernd (ed.) Mathematical Applications in Political Science 11. Dallas: Southern Methodist Univ. Press.

——— (1962b) The Theory of Political Coalitions. New Haven: Yale Univ. Press.

SCHELLING, T. C. (1960) The Strategy of Conflict. Cambridge: Harvard Univ. Press.

SHAPLEY, L. S. and M. SHUBICK (1954) "A method for evaluating the distribution of power in a committee system." American Political Science Rev. 48: 787-792.

VINACKE, W. (1954) "Sex roles in a three-person game." Sociometry 22: 343-360.

VON NEUMANN, J. and O. MORGENSTERN (1964) The Theory of Games and Economic Behavior. New York: Wiley.

ZAIS, J. P. and J. H. KESSEL. A Theory of Presidential Nominations with a 1968 Illustration. Paper delivered to the 1970 Convention of the American Political Science Association.

PAUL T. HILL is a member of the professional staff of the Research Division, National Institute of Education, Washington, D.C. He was a member of the Policy Research Division of the Office of Economic Opportunity until December, 1972, and recently served as a consultant to HUD's National Housing Subsidy Policy study. He was an American Political Science Association Congressional Fellow for the years 1968-1969. He received his Ph.D. in Political Science from Ohio State University.

A Better Way of Getting New Information

Research, survey and policy studies that say what needs to be said—no more, no less.

The Sage Papers Program

Five regularly-issued original paperback series that bring, at an unusually low cost, the timely writings and findings of the international scholarly community. Since the material is updated on a continuing basis, each series rapidly becomes a unique repository of vital information.

Authoritative, and frequently seminal, works that NEED to be available

- To scholars and practitioners
- In university and institutional libraries
- In departmental collections
- For classroom adoption

Sage Professional Papers

COMPARATIVE POLITICS SERIES
INTERNATIONAL STUDIES SERIES
ADMINISTRATIVE AND POLICY STUDIES SERIES
AMERICAN POLITICS SERIES

Sage Policy Papers

THE WASHINGTON PAPERS

SAGE PUBLICATIONS
The Publishers of Professional Social Science
Beverly Hills • London

Editors: **Harry Eckstein,** *Princeton University,* **Ted Robert Gurr,** *Northwestern University,* and **Aristide R. Zolberg,** *University of Chicago.*

SAGE PROFESSIONAL PAPERS

■ ■ ■ GENERAL INFORMATION FOR ALL FOUR SERIES

These series are designed with both research and classroom usage in mind; papers are available either on subscription (assuring quick receipt of timely work in the field – as well as savings that average between 50% and 60% off the regular single copy prices) or as single titles for personal or classroom use (priced at $2.00 to $3.00 each, depending on length). Papers range in length from 32 to 96 pages; articles are published which are too long for normal journal publication, yet too short to become books.

Frequency: twelve papers per year in each series, published in groups of four throughout the year.

Paper Edition, Unbound – Subscription Rates (for each series)

	Institutional	*Individual*
One year	$21.00/£8.00	$12.00/£5.40
Two years	$41.00/£15.50	$23.00/£10.40
Three years	$60.00/£23.00	$33.00/£15.40

Outside the U.S. and Canada, add $2.00 per year to above rates.

> Subscription discounts to professionals and students are granted ONLY on orders paid by personal check or money order. Wherever possible, payment should accompany orders, since service will not begin until payment has been received.

Bound Library Edition Available in three clothbound parts (each containing four papers) per year (in each series).

Subscription Price $30.00/£12.00 per year (i.e., $10.00/£4.00 per bound part) for each series.

Regular Price $37.50/£18.75 per annual volume (i.e., $12.50/£6.25 per bound part) – if bound parts are ordered separately, or after publication.

Outside the U.S. and Canada, add $2.00 per volume (or $.75 per part) to the above rates.

> ### What is a SAGE PROFESSIONAL PAPER?
>
> *According to CHOICE (a magazine of the American Library Association) — when reviewing our series of professional papers in comparative politics — it's a "most valuable, inexpensive . . . outlet for research products" which provides "specialists with high quality monographs too narrow and short to appear as full-length books and rather too long to be published in academic journals . . . An extremely useful library acquisition."*
> **ASK YOUR LIBRARIAN TO ORDER** *ALL* **THESE IMPORTANT SERIES TODAY !!!**

ORDER FORM

name

institution

address

city/state/zip

Please enter subscription(s) to:

☐   Prof. Pprs. in Administrative & Policy Studies

☐   Prof. Pprs. in Comparative Politics

☐   Prof. Pprs. in American Politics

☐   Prof. Pprs. in International Studies

☐   The Washington Papers

**Please send the individual papers whose numbers
I have listed below:**

☐   Please invoice (INSTITUTIONS ONLY) quot-
ing P.O. # _____ (shipping and
handling additional on non-subscription orders

☐   Payment enclosed (Sage pays shipping charges

**INSTITUTIONAL ORDERS FOR LESS THAN
$10.00 AND *ALL* PERSONAL ORDERS *MUST
BE PREPAID*. (California residents: please add
6% sales tax on non-subscription orders.)**

MAIL TO:

 **SAGE Publications, Inc. / P.O. Box 5
Beverly Hills, California 90210**
orders from the U.K., Europe, the Middle
and Africa should be sent to Sage Publicat
Ltd, 44 Hatton Garden, London EC1N 8E